Animal Show and Tell

Animals of the Night

Élisabeth de Lambilly-Bresson

GARETHSTEVENS

A Member of the WRC Media Family of Companies

The Moth

I am a moth.
I look like a butterfly,
but I am not as colorful.
I fly at night, but I like a light.
If you turn on a lamp,
I will flutter by.

The Dormouse

I am a dormouse.
I am proud
of my long, fluffy tail.
I nest in trees, among rocks,
or in attics,
where, every night,
I make lots of noise!

The Badger

I am a badger.
My striped face
is black and white.
I live in long tunnels.
I dig them all by myself
with my strong, sharp claws.
I like to eat tasty worms.
Yum!

The Owl

I am an owl.

I perch all day in a tree.

I open my big, orange eyes
when the Sun goes down.

Then I flap my huge wings
and fly away to hunt.

Whooo! Whooo! Whooo!

The Bat

I am a bat.
I sleep upside down all day.
At night, I fly away
and hunt for bugs to eat.
When I fly, I look
like a kite in the night.

The Glowworm

I am a glowworm.
I live in grass and bushes.
    In summer,
    at the end of day,
I shine a weak light.
I look like a little star
among the grass and leaves.

The Owl Monkey

I am an owl monkey.
Some call me "night monkey."
I live high in jungle trees,
where I leap
from branch to branch.
My big round eyes
help me find insects to eat.

Please visit our Web site at: www.garethstevens.com
For a free color catalog describing Gareth Stevens Publishing's
list of high-quality books and multimedia programs, call
1-800-542-2595 (USA) or 1-800-387-3178 (Canada).
Gareth Stevens Publishing's fax: (414) 332-3567.

Library of Congress Cataloging-in-Publication Data

Lambilly-Bresson, Elisabeth de.
  [Dans la nuit. English]
  Animals of the night / Elisabeth de Lambilly-Bresson. — North American ed.
    p. cm. — (Animal show and tell)
  ISBN-13: 978-0-8368-7833-2 (lib. bdg.)
  1. Nocturnal animals—Juvenile literature. I. Title.
  QL755.5.L3613 2007
  591.5'18—dc22
                           2006032931

This edition first published in 2007 by
Gareth Stevens Publishing
A Member of the WRC Media Family of Companies
330 West Olive Street, Suite 100
Milwaukee, WI 53212 USA

Translation: Gini Holland
Gareth Stevens editor: Gini Holland
Gareth Stevens art direction and design: Tammy West

This edition copyright © 2007 by Gareth Stevens, Inc. Original edition copyright © 2002 by
Mango Jeunesse Press. First published as *Les animinis: Dans la nuit* by Mango Jeunesse Press.

Printed in the United States of America

1 2 3 4 5 6 7 8 9 10 10 09 08 07 06